Harry Potter

Jokes

THE ULTIMATE JOKE

BOOK FOR WIZARDS

AND WITCHES

This document is geared towards providing exact and reliable information in regards to the topic and issue covered. The publication is sold with the idea that the publisher is not required to render an accounting, officially permitted, or otherwise, qualified services. If advice is necessary, legal or professional, a practiced individual in the profession should be ordered.

- From a Declaration of Principles which was accepted and approved equally by a

Committee of the American Bar Association and a Committee of Publishers and Associations.

The information provided herein is stated to be truthful and consistent, in that any liability, in terms of inattention or otherwise, by any usage or abuse of any

Q: On a scale of 1 to 10, how much do you like Harry Potter?

A: Approximately nine and three quarters.

Q: What's Slytherin's Favourite Subject?

A: Hissssstory

Q: What kind of cereal do they serve at Hogwarts?

A: Hufflepuffs

Q: Why did Barty Crouch Jr. quit drinking?

A: Because it was making him Moody.

Q: Why is Mad-Eye Moody such a bad teacher?

A: Because he can't control his pupils.

Q: Why does Voldemort use Twitter and not Facebook?

A: Because he only has followers, not friends.

Q: Why does Neville have to use two bathroom stalls?

A: Because of his Longbottom.

Q: Why did Lucius Malfoy cross the road twice?

A: Because he's a double crosser.

Q: What do you call two quidditch players who share the same room?

A: Broom-mates

Q: How do you get a mythical creature into your room?

A: Through the Gryffindor

Q: How do Malfoys enter a building?

A: They Slytherin.

Q: Why did Snape stand in the middle of the road?

A: So you never know what side he is on.

Q: Why can't Harry tell apart his best friend and his potions equipment?

A: Because they're both cauldron.

Q: You don't like my jokes?

A: There must be something Ron with you.

Q: Why was Harry sent to the Headmaster's office?

A: Because he was cursing in class.

Q: Why doesn't Voldemort have glasses?

A: Nobody nose.

Q: How does Harry get rid of an itch?

A: With Quit-itch

Q: What did the comedian say to Harry?

A: Why so Sirius?

Q: Why did the Death Eaters cross the road?

A: Because the Dark Lord ordered it.

Q: How do the Death Eaters freshen their breath?

A: With Dementos

Q: What is Big Foot's favourite book?

A: Hairy Potter

Q: Did you survive Avada Kedavra?

A: Cause you're drop dead gorgeous.

Q: Why did the witch drop out of Hogwarts to travel?

A: Because she had Wand-erlust

Q: Why didn't Harry like the Triwizard Tournament?

A: Because it was dragon on and on.

Q: What do you call the star student in Professor Sprout's class?

A: Herb

Q: What happened to Draco's plan to get back at Harry?

A: It was Malfoyled.

Q: How does Harry's best friend do his exercise?

A: He Rons.

Q: Why does Ron have such a hard time studying?

A: He lacked hocus focus.

Q: Does Ron have a chance of being at the top of his class?

A: Where there's a quill, there's a way.

Q: Did you hear about Percy Weasley?

A: I heard he's the perfect prefect.

Q: Why did Draco avoid Hermione?

A: Because his parents told him not to talk to Grangers.

Q: Are you sure you know what Hermione's Patronus is?

A: You otter.

Q: Do you know Ron's Patronus?

A: It would be terrier if you didn't.

Q: Where do Hermione's parents live?

A: Back on the Grange.

Q: What do Harry and Ron have in common?

A: One had a scar and the other had Scabbers.

Q: Where can you find Dumbledore's army?

A: Up his sleevy.

Q: Do wizards who drink Polyjuice Potion have feelings?

A: Of course. They're people two.

Q: When do Slytherin's eat cake?

A: When it's time for dessssssert.

Q: What can you do that Voldemort can't?

A: Sneeze

Q: What would you get Voldemort on Valentine's Day?

A: A bouquet of followers.

Q: What kind of stories do Voldemort's minions tell?

A: Worm-tales

Q: How do two Slytherins show that they like each other?

A: They give each other a little hiss.

Q: Who is Slytherin's favourite rapper?

A: Drake-o

Q: What does Draco Malfoy have for breakfast?

A: Dracon and Eggs

Q: Why does Voldemort love Nagini?

A: Because she gives him lots of hugs and hisses.

Having some good laughs?

Leave a review and let us know what joke you like the most so far!

Did you know that... Dumbledore and Harry are the only two known wizards who have been in possession of all 3 Deathly Hallows at one time, effectively making them the masters of death according to legend.

Q: What's Slytherin's favourite dance?

A: The Mamba

Q: Which Professor at Hogwarts gets blamed for everything?

A: Professor Snape Goat

Q: How many wizards does it take to change a lightbulb?

A: None. Wizards don't use electricity.

Q: Why wouldn't Ron's car move?

A: Because it got stuck in a Quidditch.

Q: Why did Voldemort cross the road?

A: Because Harry couldn't stop him.

Q: Why was Draco's shirt covered in mud?

A: Because he spent the day Slytherin.

Q: What did Harry say when Hermione didn't like his joke?

A: What's Ron with you.

Q: What did Ron say to Harry when he found his missing wand?

A: Wanderful!

Q: Can you tell the difference between Fred and George Weasley?

A: I can't tell which is witch.

Q: How do Hogwarts students travel on field trips?

A: They Albus.

Q: What is a common pastime at Hogwarts?

A: Trying to solve the Rubeus cube.

Q: What did Harry Potter wear when his hair fell out?

A: A Hedwig.

Q: What should you do if you have a question about jail?

A: Azkaban

Q: What did Fluffy say when he sat on sandpaper?

A: Ruff ruff!

Q: What type of markets does Fluffy avoid?

A: Flea markets

Q: Why did Crabbe and Goyle cross the road?

A: Because Draco did.

Q: Which minister of magic has a car named after him?

A: Prius Thicknesse

Q: What's Hagrid's favourite dessert?

A: Black Forest Cake

Q: What is the name of the wizard making evil plans?

A: Harry Plotter

Q: What do Death Eaters eat for breakfast?

A: Cruci-os

Q: Why does Dobby always criticize himself?

A: He has low elf esteem.

Q: What do you call a Hogwarts headmaster who can't speak clearly?

A: Mumbledore.

Q: How did Hedwig react when Voldemort showed up?

A: She didn't give a hoot.

Q: What did Voldemort say when Wormtail asked if he could really rise again?

A: He replied yes, but you might have to give me a hand.

Q: If Hermione was abandoned, what would she be called?

A: The Lone Granger.

Q: What was Voldemort's Parents' favourite game?

A: "I Got Your Nose"

Q: What do you call a Hufflepuff that works out?

A: Hufflebuff

Q: Why did the Weasley cross the road?

A: Because he saw a Knut.

Q: What do you call a wizard who's good at math?

A: A math wiz.

Q: What did Voldemort get when he rolled the dice?

A: Snake eyes

Q: What kind of drinks do magical parrots like?

A: Pollyjuice potions

Q: Why doesn't Snape teach Herbology?

A: Because his lilly died.

Q: Why is Herbology Slytherin's favourite class?

A: Because it's in the greenhouse.

Q: What's a good place to buy Horcruxes?

A: At Voldamart.

Q: What do you call a Potterhead on a horse?

A: Harry Trotter

Q: Why did Trevor cross the road?

A: To get away from Longbottom.

Q: Why did the Quidditch player travel on a broom?

A: Because he didn't have a vacuum cleaner.

Q: How do you know if someone is a pureblood at Hogwarts?

A: Don't worry they'll let you know.

Yo momma's so fat the Sorting Hat put her in all the houses.

Yo momma's so fat her Patronus is a milkshake.

Yo momma's so ugly not even a Dementor would give her a kiss.

Yo momma's so fat even Wingardium Leviosa couldn't lift her.

Yo momma so fat she tried to eat Cornelius Fudge.

Yo momma so fat, her boggart turns into a treadmill.

Yo momma so ugly that when she walked into Gringotts Bank, they gave her a job application.

Yo momma so ugly that the Basilisk turned to stone when he looked at her. Roses are red, violets are blue, I thought Voldemort was ugly, but then I saw you.

After Order of the Phoenix, things started to get dead Sirius.

Harry your godfather is dead.

You can't be Sirius.

I'm dead Sirius.

Harry is sliding down that hill. JK he's Rowling.

Voldemort: Why so Sirius?

Sirius Black: Why so nosy?

Snape: Voldemort is coming!

Harry: Are you Sirius?

Snape: No I'm Severus.

Knock knock.

Who's there?

Harry.

Harry who?

Harry up and let us in, Voldemort's coming.

Knock knock.

Who's there?

Sirius.

Sirius who?

Sirius-ly open the door!

Knock knock.

Who's there?

Draco.

Draco who?

Draco lot of water. Can I use the bathroom?

Knock knock.

Who's there?

Albus look both ways before you cross the street.

Knock knock

who's there?

Ron.

Ron who?

Ron for your life. Voldemort is coming.

Knock knock.

Who's there?

Dobby.

Dobby who?

Do-bby silly, it's just me.

Well done on getting through all the jokes!

If you enjoyed the jokes and had enough laughs to make Voldemort wail then feel free to leave a review and let us know which one you laughed at the most!

As a special thank you for purchasing this book, enjoy these bonus Harry Potter facts from one of our other best selling titles!

1. Ageing Potion vs Dumbledore's Age Line

In the Goblet of Fire, Fred and George Weasley attempt to manipulate their ages by drinking an Ageing Potion so they can enter into the Triwizard Tournament. Dumbledore's spell, however, is strong enough to detect the potion thus failing the boys' attempt into beating the system.

2. Voldemort's Inability to Love

Since Voldemort's father was under the effects of a Love Potion when Voldemort was born, the Dark Lord is unable to feel any love. Any child born while one of their parent is under the effects of a Love Potion will be unable to feel any love since the love of one of the parents is forced.

3.   Boggarts

Boggarts are shape-shifting creates that take the form of whatever is scariest to the person in front of them. In other words, they take shape of your worst fear. The more fearful you are as a person, the more susceptible you are to Boggarts since they are attracted to fear.

4. Voldemort's Greatest Fear and his Boggart's Form

Voldemort's greatest fear is his own death which is why he created so many Horcruxes. Therefore, if a Boggart were to appear in front of him, it would take the form of Voldemort's corpse. This has been confirmed by J.K. Rowling.

5. I open at the close

This phrase appears on the golden snitch that Dumbledore passes on to Harry. It comes from the fact that the Harry Potter and the Philosopher's Stone (the first book in the series) was published in 1998 which is the year the Battle of Hogwarts, the final battle in the series, took place.

6. Professor Trelawney's Curse

A Seer is someone who is able to see into the future through supernatural means. Professor Trelawney's great great grandmother was a pure Seer but her gift was diluted over the generations and was not as strong in her great great granddaughter. In Greek mythology, a Seer named Cassandra was put under a curse which made no one believe in her prophecies. Similarly in the series, no one believed Professor Trelawney's prophecies.

7.   The Mirror of Erised

The Mirror shows a person their strongest wishes. When Harry stands in front of the Mirror, he sees his family alive and reunited. Dumbledore sees the same thing as Harry since his family was also torn apart. Erised is simply desire spelled backwards.

8.   Went Down Laughing

Sirius Black and Fred Weasley were both infamous pranksters in their days at Hogwarts and both died laughing even as they were taken down.

9. Dudley's Magical Child

J.K. Rowling has said that she almost wrote Dudley, Harry's Muggle cousin, into the epilogue, standing at Platform 9 ¾ with a magical child. She changed her mind however, mentioning that "any latent wizarding genes would never survive contact with Uncle Vernon's DNA."

10. The Patronus Prediction

Ron's Patronus is a Jack Russell terrier while Hermione's is an otter. Jack Russell terriers are known to chase otters. This is most likely a foreshadowing of Ron eventually marrying Hermione.

11. No More Patronus Charms

After his twin brother Fred's death, George Weasley was unable to summon a Patronus ever again. Since Patronus charms require a wizard to conjure up their happiest memories in order to give it power, it is likely that George had gone into depression meaning he could not feel enough happy emotions to cast the charm.

12. Headmaster Snape's Portrait

Since Snape had abandoned his post as Headmaster of Hogwarts, his portrait was not hung in the Headmaster's Office. Harry, however, changed that and had it hung to honor Snape's sacrifice and dedication to defeating Voldemort.

13. Leaving the Same Way I Came In

Harry Potter was dropped off as a baby to 4 Privet Drive, the home of his Aunt Petunia and Uncle Vernon, by Hagrid on Sirius Black's motorcycle. At the end of the series, he leaves in the same motorcycle with Hagrid.

14. What Could Have Been

According to Rowling, Lily Potter (then Lily Evans) could have fallen in love with Snape if he had not chosen to pursue the Dark Arts.

However, this potentially means we would have had a Harry Snape instead of a Harry Potter!

15. Gandalf the Grey

In Harry Potter and the Chamber of Secrets, a picture of Gandalf the Grey from Lord of the Rings can be seen in a Collection of Great Wizards book in Dumbledore's study. This is a tribute to Gandalf who is considered one of the most iconic wizards in modern literature.

16. Dumbledore's Crush

Dumbledore, one of the most powerful wizards of all time, was gay as revealed by J.K.

Rowling. He had a crush on Grindelwald who he grew up with as a teenage boy. However, it is unclear whether Grindelwald shared the same feelings toward Dumbledore.

17. Finish Your Homework, Kids!

During the scenes in which Harry, Ron and Hermione can be seen doing schoolwork, they were actually doing their own real homework from school. That goes to show that even child actors in the biggest movies still have to finish their homework!

18. You're an Actor, Hagrid!

Robbie Coltrane who plays Rubeus Hagrid in the films was the first actor to be cast. This is most likely because of the size requirement needed to play the character which narrowed down the number of characters who could actually play him.

19. The 7 Hedwigs

A total of 7 owls played the role of Hedwig in the films with 3 being in the first film alone. The names of these owls are Gizmo, Kasper, Oops, Swoops, Oh Oh, Elmo, and Bandit.

20. Harry's Scar

In the books, Harry's scar is in the middle of his forehead while in the films, it is more off to the side. Rowling specifically requested this to be changed for the film adaptation most likely to make it more of a subtle detail.

21. Float Like a Butterfly, Sting Like a Bumblebee?

Dumbledore in Old English means bumblebee. Rowling said it brought her joy to imagine Albus wandering around the castle humming like a bee.

22. Moaning Myrtle's Real Age

The actress who portrayed Moaning Myrtle was actually 37 years old and was the oldest actor/actress to portray a Hogwarts student (both past and present) in the series.

23. If J.K. Rowling were in the Wizarding World

When asked what she would teach if she were a professor at Hogwarts, Rowling said she instruct Charms class. If she had to choose a specific job, she would be an author of spell books, which makes sense since she is an author!

24. Symbols of Depression

Dementors were created based on Rowling's own battles with depression. She explained depression as a "cold absence of feeling – that really hollowed out feeling. That's what Dementors are." This also explains why they can be expelled by Patronus charms. If depression is the absence of happy feeling then being struck by intense happiness is the counter.

25. Hermione's Buck Teeth

Emma Watson originally had to wear buck teeth in the film to make her look like how she was described in the books. However, she could not talk properly with them on so they were taken out.

26. Alan Rickman the Master of Secrets

To help him prepare for his role as Severus Snape, Rowling revealed many spoilers to Alan. Many of these were not told to anyone else until the final book was published.

27. The Many Uses of Dragon Blood

Albus Dumbledore wrote about the 12 Uses of Dragon Blood but the only ones revealed to us are that it is a surprisingly effective oven cleaner and spot remover.

28. Back on the New York Bestseller List

The Harry Potter books were the first children's books to make the list since Charlotte's Web in 1952.

29. The Craze for Harry Potter

There was so much demand and craze for the series that when Harry Potter and the Prisoner of Azkaban was to be released, the publisher asked that the books not be sold until after schools were closed for the day in order to prevent children from skipping class.

30. Harry's Green Eyes

Similar to Emma Watson's buck teeth failure, Daniel Radcliffe was given green contact lenses to match his appearance in the books, but he had an allergic reaction to the lenses. They cancelled the green eyes and proceeded.

Be sure to check out our other great Harry Potter titles by searching "<u>Lilly Winchester</u>" on Amazon!

Made in the USA
Monee, IL
08 November 2019

16497126R00036